The Anglo-Saxons Resource Book

Contents

Anglo-Saxons and Roman-Britons

Who were the Anglo-Saxons?

These are pirates attacking Britain at the time of
the Romans. The pirates were Saxons.
They came in boats across the North Sea from their
homes in Germany, and raided villas and
villages near the sea. They stole food, gold and silver.
Then they sailed away again.

Drawing by Alan Sorrell

Find:

- The Saxon boats. How many are there?

- Saxons pulling their boat ashore and
  bringing in their oars.

- The Roman signal station on the cliff.

- The smoke signal.

- The messenger riding off on horseback.

- Another signal station further up the coast.

The Saxons used boats like this one. It held between sixty and eighty people and it needed about thirty people to row it.

Archaeologists found this boat over a hundred years ago in a peat bog at Nydam in Denmark. The Saxons built it with oak planks.

Find:
• The rudder.
• The slots for the oars to pull against.

Archaeologist
Someone who finds out about the past from clues buried under the ground.

Many of these boats sank on the crossing to Britain. Why do you think that was?

This map shows you where the Anglo-Saxons lived and how they gradually took over Britain.

Three other tribes lived close to the Saxons. They were the Angles, the Frisians and the Jutes.

We usually call all these tribes Anglo Saxons.

The Anglo-Saxons were farmers as well as sailors. They found it difficult to grow enough food on their own land because it was covered with woods and marshes.

When they heard from the raiding parties that there was plenty of good land in Britain, they decided to go and settle there.

Scots
Britons
NORTH SEA
Jutes
Angles
Saxons
Frisians
Britons or Welsh
Britons or Welsh
Germany

Anglo Saxons 5th Century

Anglo Saxons 7th Century

Britons

The Roman-Britons and the Invasion

When the Romans ruled Britain, people lived in towns as well as on farms and in **villas** in the country. This is the town of Wroxeter at about the time the Saxon raids began.

Drawing by Alan Sorrell

Villa

A big country house made of stone and wood with a tiled roof. It was usually on one floor like a bungalow. The owner ran a big farm on the land around it.

Find:
- The town wall.
- The buildings. What are they made of?

Do you think life in Wroxeter was fairly safe and comfortable? How can you tell?

The Roman-Britons wanted to keep the **raiders** out so they built forts by the sea and signal towers to warn people.
Here is one of the forts.
The Romans built this fort at Porchester, near Portsmouth.
Some of the buildings in the middle were added in later times.

Raiders

People who make a sudden attack on a place, stealing and causing damage.

Many other tribes as well as the Anglo-Saxons wanted to live inside the Roman Empire, because there seemed to be plenty of land and people were rich.

The Romans did not want to let them in, so the tribes attacked. In the end the emperor decided he needed the Roman army in Britain to go to defend other parts of the **empire**.

The Roman-Britons were frightened. A tribe from Ireland, called the Scots, and one from Scotland, called the Picts, were attacking them in the north. They begged the emperor to send soldiers back to defend them. But he said they would have to look after themselves.

They decided to pay some of the Anglo-Saxons to come over and help them against the invaders in the north. Afterwards the Anglo-Saxon chiefs refused to go home.

More and more Anglo-Saxons arrived. They sailed up rivers and settled on the land beside them. Then they started to spread out across Britain.

Sometimes the Roman-Britons carried on living next to them. Sometimes they fought to keep them away. The Anglo-Saxons were strong fighters. In the end they managed to take over all the land except in Wales, Devon and Cornwall.

> **Empire**
> A group of countries ruled by one country.

Anglo-Saxon fighters.

They all used spears and shields.

The richer ones also had helmets and swords. Swords were very valuable and often handed down from father to son.

Where the Anglo-Saxons Settled

The Anglo-Saxons gave names to the places where they settled. We still use many of them today. If a place has an Anglo-Saxon name it means they lived there.

So place-names are the best clue to where the Anglo-Saxons settled.

Here are some of the names they used and what they mean.

This is a map of part of Cambridgeshire. How many Anglo-Saxon names can you find on it?

Look at a map of the area where you live and see if you can find any Anglo-Saxon names.

den, dene	=	valley
feld, field	=	field
ford	=	shallow river crossing
ham	=	settlement
ing	=	the people of (Reading, in Berkshire, was the place of the people of Reada, their leader)
lea, leigh	=	clearing in the woods
ton	=	farm or village
wick, wich, wic	=	farmstead
worth	=	land with a hedge round it

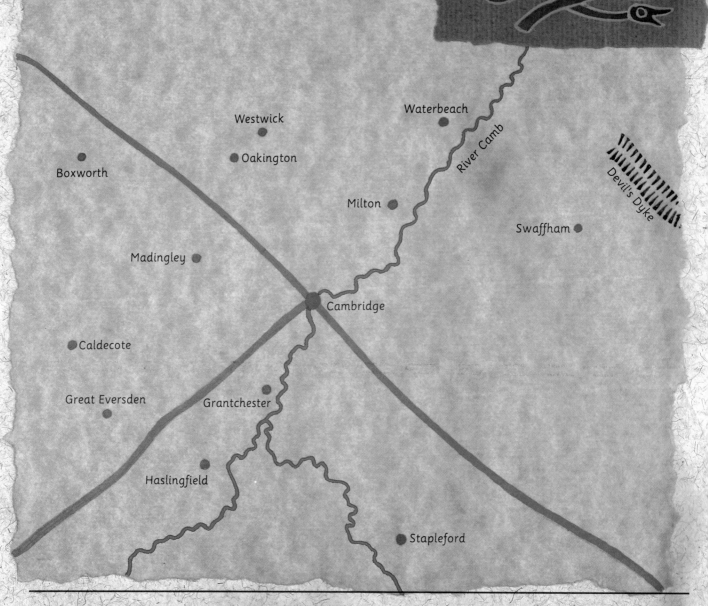

The Anglo-Saxons built their houses out of wood, clay and straw so they rotted away long ago. But sometimes a photograph like this, taken from an aeroplane, shows marks on the ground that are clues that the Anglo-Saxons once lived there.

The white marks show where houses once stood.

This is how the first Anglo-Saxon **settlements** probably looked. As you can see they were very different to a Roman-British town like Wroxeter.

Settlement

A place where people settle and live.

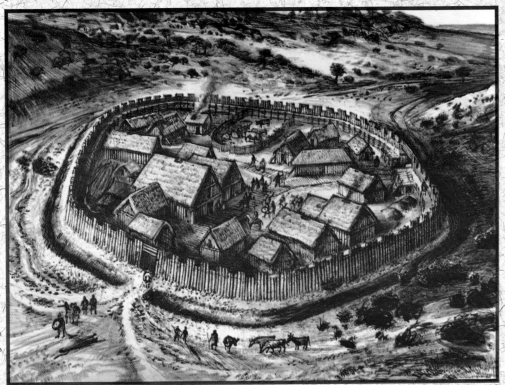

Drawing by Alan Sorrell

Find:
- The houses and workshops.
- The paths. What are they made of?
- The fenced-in space for animals.
- The wall and ditch. What do you think they are for?

The Anglo-Saxons called their part of Britain 'Engle-land' and started to call themselves the 'Englisc'. The English language spoken today comes from their language.

But England was not one country like it is now. To begin with there were lots of separate Anglo-Saxon kingdoms with their own rulers.

A Royal Grave

Just over fifty years ago, in 1939, archaeologists found the grave of the ruler of one of the first Anglo-Saxon kingdoms. It was under a grass-covered mound of sand at a place called Sutton Hoo, in Suffolk.

This is what they found when they dug into the mound.

It was the remains of an enormous ship. Inside were many things belonging to the dead king. The archaeologists did not find the remains of the dead king's body. They think it rotted completely away.

This photograph was taken in 1939, when most people still used black and white film. The ship was built from wooden planks held together with iron nails. They all rotted away but you can see the prints they left in the sand.

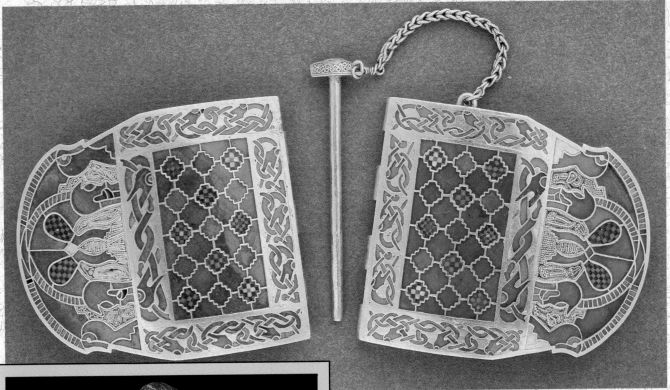

These are the gold shoulder-clasps that the king used to hold together the front and back parts of his leather coat of armour.

Find:
- The two clasps. They are curved to fit the shoulders. There is a clip on the back of each one to hold it to the leather.

- The pin. It fits through holes on the back of the clasps to make them into a hinge.

- The pattern of animals twisted together round the squares.

- The patterns of two wild pigs on the curved ends of each clasp. The pigs are facing each other. Their curly tails are on the outside.

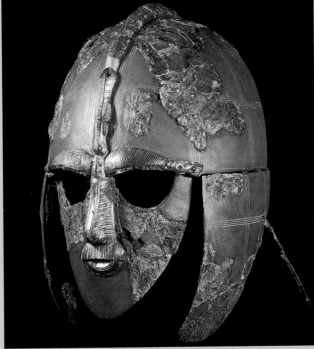

The archaeologists found lots of small bits of the king's helmet. They pieced them together to show how it probably looked.

The helmet was made of iron covered with bronze stamped with patterns and pictures.

Find:
- The hinged flaps to protect the ears and neck.
- The animal heads at the end of the eye brows.
- The jewels below them.
- The patterns on the nose and moustache.

Do you think this king was a rich man?

Do you think some of the Anglo-Saxons were clever artists?

How can you tell?

Houses and Home Life

Villagers

The Anglo-Saxons lived in villages. Ordinary villagers lived in houses like these. Archaeologists built them at West Stow in Suffolk where there was once an Anglo-Saxon village. They used the clues they found there to work out how to do it.

Find:
- The wooden walls.
- The thatched roofs.

Here is a picture of one of the clues. It is the place where a house once stood. There is a pit dug in the ground and some holes at each end. How many holes are there?

This is how the archaeologists think the Anglo-Saxons built the house using the pit and the holes at each end.

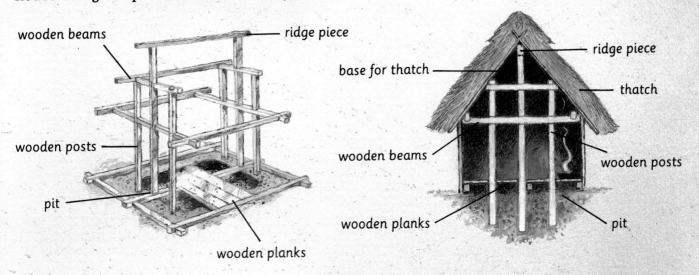

wooden beams — ridge piece

wooden posts

pit

wooden planks

base for thatch — ridge piece

thatch

wooden beams

wooden posts

wooden planks — pit

thatch

beams

plank walls

door

This sort of house was probably used for a family to live in, or sometimes as a place to make or store things. It had one room with a space under the floor.

The archaeologists also found another sort of building at West Stow. It still had one room but it was bigger and it had a place for a fire in the middle of the floor. The Anglo-Saxons called this a hall. Several families, who were related to each other, shared one hall. They used it as a place to meet and for eating together.

These people have dressed up to show how the Anglo-Saxon villagers of West Stow may have looked about five hundred years after the first settlers arrived.

Find:
- **The two women on their way to fetch water.**
- **Their dresses. Each of them is wearing a woollen dress over a linen one.**
- **Their head-coverings.**
- **The man chopping wood.**
- **His shirt or cyrtle. It is long so he uses a belt to hold it up in a fold.**
- **The man with the child.**
- **His cloak fastened at the shoulder.**
- **His trousers.**
- **The villagers wove their clothes themselves and dyed them different colours. How many colours can you find?**

Most villagers were free people. That meant they owned their house and some land and they could move to another village if they wished. But some of them were **slaves**. Look at the picture again. The man up the ladder is a slave who has been told to mend a roof.

Slaves

People who had to work for other people without having any wages. They could be sold by their owners to someone else.

The villagers made some of the tools they needed out of wood or bone. They also had iron tools such as axes and **ploughshares**.

These bone combs were found at West Stow.
Find the patterns on them.

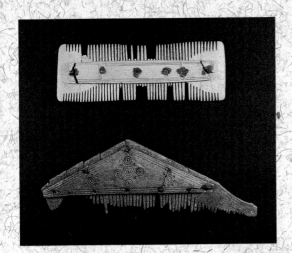

Ploughshares

The ploughshare is the part of the plough that cuts the earth.

Men and women used brooches to fasten their clothes.

These come from West Stow. They are made from a mixture of copper and tin called bronze.

Women liked to wear long strings of beads made of glass or a stone called amber.

Sometimes they wore them round the waist.

Thanes and Ladies

The Anglo-Saxons called the lords who owned a lot of land 'thanes'.

A thane. An Anglo-Saxon monk painted this picture in a book.

Find the thane's:

• **Sword and sheath (for holding it by his side).**

• **Cloak.**

• **Tunic.**

• **Trousers.**

• **Garters (bands of leather) and shoes.**

What are the clues that he is a wealthy person?

The villagers who lived on a thane's land had to swear to be loyal to him and fight for him if he needed them.

Thanes had to swear to be loyal to the king and to take their villagers to fight for him if he asked. Thanes lived in bigger houses than villagers.

The richest and most important thanes were called 'eaorls' or earls. Some earls had houses as big as this palace which belonged to a king.

Drawing by Alan Sorrell

This painting shows how the artist thinks the royal palace at Cheddar in Somerset probably looked.
Find:

• **The main building or hall.**

• **The stone church.**

The Anglo-Saxons called a wealthy woman like this a 'lady'.

Some ladies owned their own house and land and organised everything themselves. A lady who was married to a thane organised what had to be done in their house and helped him to run their lands.

These are 'girdle hangers'. Archaeologists often find them in the graves of better off Anglo-Saxon women. Wealthy women often wore them in pairs hanging from the girdle, or belt, round their gowns. They are made of bronze and shaped like keys. They were a sign that the woman was in charge of her family's stores and money.

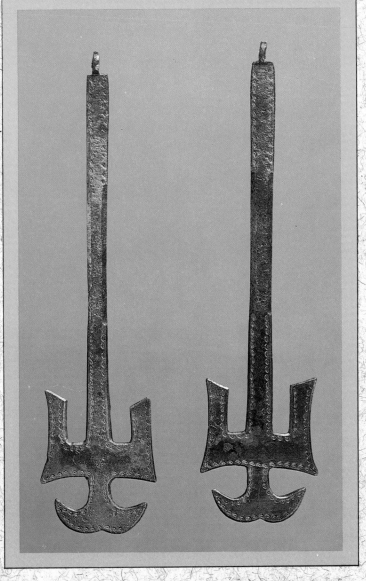

This picture comes from a book made by a monk.
Find:
- The woman's gown held at the waist by a girdle or belt.

- Her cloak.

- Her head-covering.

Food and Feasting

Villagers ate bread, vegetables and eggs, as well as the fish and birds which they caught. Most of them kept animals, so they ate meat sometimes too. They drank ale, a weak beer, which they made themselves.

Rich families ate the same things, but they had more of everything, especially meat. They also drank wine and mead, a strong drink made from honey and water.

All Anglo-Saxons liked to give feasts in their hall. When a thane gave a feast, his family and important guests sat at the top table. Less important people sat on benches and tables further down the hall.

This is the top table at a feast.
Find:
- **The servants kneeling by the table offering meat cooked on skewers.**

- **The knives and a spoon. They did not use forks.**

- **The bread in bowls.**

During the feast a musician called a 'minstrel' played the harp and sang songs for the guests.
This minstrel is playing a small harp called a 'lyre'.

The Anglo-Saxons were fond of music. How many different instruments can you find in this picture?

Rich Anglo-Saxons could afford expensive things to use at their dining table. This is a drinking horn.

The horn is from a cow.
The metal parts are silver
and gold.
Find the patterns on them.

This is a glass beaker.

Beakers like this were
made in Germany.
They are called 'claw
beakers.' Why do you
think this is?

Work and Trade

Work on the Land

The Anglo-Saxons lived by
farming the land.
The villagers had special jobs
to do in each season of the year.
In the autumn they had
to plough the land and sow the
wheat and barley seeds.

Ploughing

In the winter there wasn't enough food for all the animals, so the Anglo-Saxons had to kill some of them. They ate the meat and made clothes from the skins. In the spring they sowed peas and beans to eat in the summer.

In June they mowed the grass in the village meadow by the stream. This gave them hay to feed some of the animals next winter.

Some villagers had special jobs. This is the shepherd.

In August they cut the wheat and barley and beat it to separate out the grain. They used most of the grain to make bread and ale and kept some to sow for next year.

Weaving

The villagers spun the wool from their sheep into thread like this.

They held the wool in one hand and pulled out a thread.

Then they fixed it to a stick or spindle which was spun between the fingers and twisted the wool into a long thread.

A weight with a hole in the middle, called a spindle-whorl, fitted over the stick and helped to spin it.

They wound the thread onto the spindle as they went along.

Then they wove the thread into cloth for clothes.
This is the sort of loom the villagers used for weaving.
It leant against the wall of the house.

Here are some things used for making cloth that archaeologists found in West Stow.

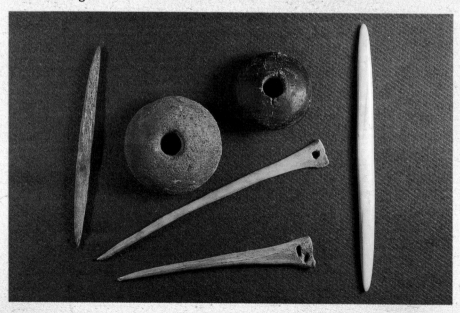

Find:
- The bone pins and needles.
- The two round weights are clay spindle whorls.

Women did most of the spinning and weaving. Some women were also very good at sewing pictures on cloth using coloured thread. Pictures made like this are called 'embroidery'.

You can still see this piece of Anglo-Saxon embroidery in Durham **Cathedral**.

How many different coloured threads can you find?

Cathedral

The chief church in an area. It is usually very big.

Making and Trading

Some Anglo-Saxons made their living by making things that people needed.

This is a smith. He was one of the most important people in the village. He made iron blades for tools such as ploughshares, spades and scythes. He also made blades for swords and the points for spears.

**What is the smith doing?
What tools is he using?**

Here are some other things he made.

Find:
- **The key.**
- **The punch.**
- **The shears.**

Some people made brooches, buckles and jewellery. They made them out of bronze for the villagers. Richer people could afford expensive things such as these gold clasps.

Archaeologists found these clasps in the grave of an Anglo-Saxon chief in Taplow, in Buckinghamshire. They were part of his sword belt.
Find the patterns on them.

This picture shows builders
and carpenters at work.

A monk painted this picture.
The building is in the clouds.
Perhaps it is meant to be
in Heaven. Can you see another
clue about that?
How many different tools
can you find?
What are they for?

The people of some villages became well known for making
things. So other people came to buy them in the market.
Those villages grew bigger and became small towns.

This is part of the town
of Thetford, in Suffolk.

The artist used clues found at
Thetford by archaeologists to
paint this picture.

Find:
- The people at the well.

- The carts.

- The rubbish pits.

- Travellers on the road. It is
  really a mud track.

- Animals. How many different
  kinds are there? What clues
  about animals do you think
  the archaeologists found?

Drawing by Alan Sorrell

The people of Thetford were well known for making clay pots like this. They sent them all over the country.

This picture shows the kind of cart they probably used to carry the pots.

Find:

- The cart.

- The wheels with wooden spokes.

- The oxen. How many pull each cart?

- The wooden collars, called 'yokes', to keep each pair of oxen together.

- The driver with a long stick.

Look at the picture of Thetford again. How do you think the artist knew how to draw the cart?

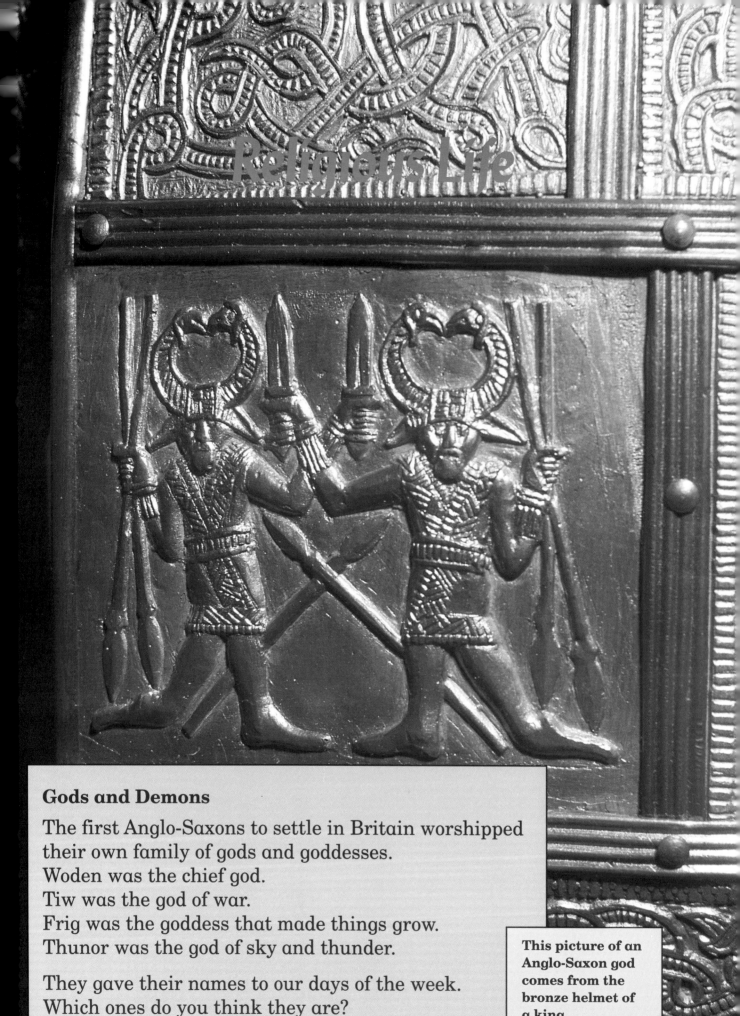

Gods and Demons

The first Anglo-Saxons to settle in Britain worshipped their own family of gods and goddesses.

Woden was the chief god.

Tiw was the god of war.

Frig was the goddess that made things grow.

Thunor was the god of sky and thunder.

They gave their names to our days of the week. Which ones do you think they are?

This picture of an Anglo-Saxon god comes from the bronze helmet of a king.

The first settlers believed in magic powers. Rich people wore rings like this to keep away sickness and danger.

Look at the signs on the ring. They are letters, called 'runes' which the Anglo-Saxons used for writing. Sometimes they used runes to make patterns which they thought had magic powers.

They also believed in elves and demons.

When they had a pain they thought it was because the elves and demons were shooting arrows at them.

An attack by elves and demons.

Christianity

At the time of the Anglo-Saxon invasions, Christianity was the religion of everyone in the Roman Empire. That meant they believed in the life and teachings of Jesus Christ.

So the Roman-Britons were Christians, but the Anglo-Saxons were not. As the Anglo-Saxons settled, many of the Roman-Britons moved away. Christianity slowly disappeared except in Cornwall, Wales and Scotland where the Roman-Britons still lived.

Even though Christianity disappeared in much of England, it lived on in Rome, the home of the chief Christian **priest**, called the 'Pope'.

> ### Priest
>
> Someone with the special job of looking after other Christians, teaching them about Jesus, and leading church services.

This picture shows Pope Gregory.

He became Pope about two hundred years after the Anglo-Saxons started to settle in Britain.

Pope Gregory decided to try to persuade the Anglo-Saxons to become Christians. So he sent some **monks** to England led by a man called Augustine.

> ### Monks
>
> Men who live together in monasteries. They have to promise to stay poor, not to get married, and to spend their lives praying to God. Women who do this are called 'nuns'.

Augustine first went to talk to Aethelberht, king of the Anglo-Saxons in Kent. Aethelberht's wife, Bertha, came from France. She was already a Christian. So the king welcomed Augustine and allowed him to use an old Roman church in Canterbury.

Soon Aethelberht and many of his people became Christians. Pope Gregory made Augustine 'Archbishop of Canterbury', which meant he was in charge of all the Christians in England.

Monks and priests started to travel all over England. They often had crosses like this put up. People went there to hear them talk about Jesus.

You can still see this stone cross in Bewcastle in Cumbria. The top part has broken off. Find the carvings on the sides.

As more Anglo-Saxons became Christians they started to build churches. They mostly used wood. Today this church still has the walls which the Anglo-Saxons made from tree-trunks.

This church is at Greensted in Essex. Most of the Anglo-Saxon wooden churches have rotted away.

About the time the first Anglo-Saxons settled in England a Roman-British monk called Patrick went to Ireland. Many Irish people became Christian because of his teaching.

Thirty years before Augustine arrived in England from Rome, an Irish monk, called Columba, sailed from Ireland to Iona, a small island off the coast of Scotland. There he built a monastery, which is a place for monks to live and pray to God.

This is the monastery on Iona today.

Columba and his monks built a wooden church and wooden huts to live in. They have all rotted away.

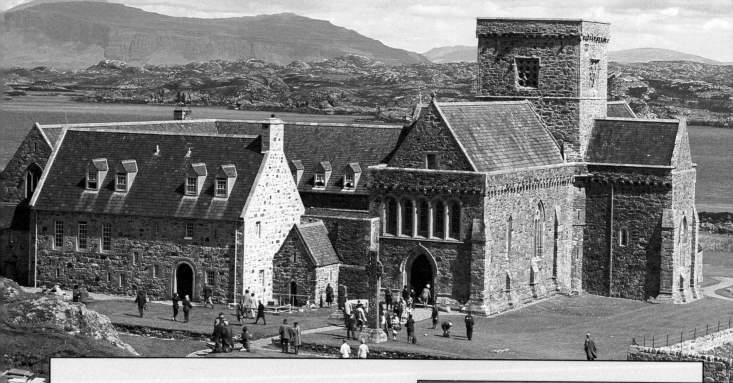

Oswald, the Anglo-Saxon king of Northumbria, was a Christian and he once stayed with the monks at Iona. He asked them to come to teach his people about Christianity. So some of them went to Northumbria and built a monastery on the island of Lindisfarne, just off the coast. From there the monks went all over the north of England telling people about Jesus.

This is Lindisfarne today. The first monastery has disappeared. The ruins you can see are the remains of another monastery that was built hundreds of years later in 1095 AD.

The monks at Lindisfarne copied books out by hand and decorated them. This is a page from the Lindisfarne Gospels. The gospels are the books written by the followers of Jesus to tell the story of his life.

This is the first page of St Luke's Gospel.
Find:

- The different patterns. How many are there?

- The birds and animals in the patterns. How many can you see?

- The letters.

Monks and Nuns

When the Anglo-Saxons became Christians many of them decided to become monks or nuns.

People who became monks or nuns were taught to read and write Latin as well as Anglo-Saxon.

This picture shows a monk giving some nuns a book he has written in Latin specially for them.

These nuns lived in Barking Abbey. Their abbess was called Hildelith. Find her at the back. What clues are there in this picture that some monks and nuns probably led quite comfortable lives even though they promised to be poor?

Women from noble families often became nuns. Some of them became the '**abbess**'.

One famous abbess was called Hild. She was very clever and wise. Anglo-Saxon kings used to ask her for advice.

Abbess

An abbess was in charge of an abbey or nunnery where nuns lived.

Here is a monk working in his study.
He is writing or drawing with a pen.

Find:
- The monk's books on the shelf in the cupboard at the back.
- His pen. It is a quill pen, made from a bird's feather.
- The ink in a pot on the table.

Many monks became teachers and writers. One of the best known was called Bede. His parents sent him to live with monks when he was only seven. They taught him to read and write.

Then he joined a monastery at Jarrow and lived there for the rest of his life.

He wrote many books. The most famous was *A History of the English Church and People*. We still use it today to find out about Anglo-Saxon times.

Rulers and Kingdoms

King Offa

An Anglo-Saxon king called Offa wanted to mark the line between his kingdom, called 'Mercia', and the land of the Britons who lived in Wales. So he ordered this great ditch and bank to be built.

It is called 'Offa's dyke'. You can still see it today. It is 148 miles, or 238 kilometres long.

Offa was a very powerful king. He had coins made with his picture on them. This is one of them.

Find the letters on the coin that spell OFFA.

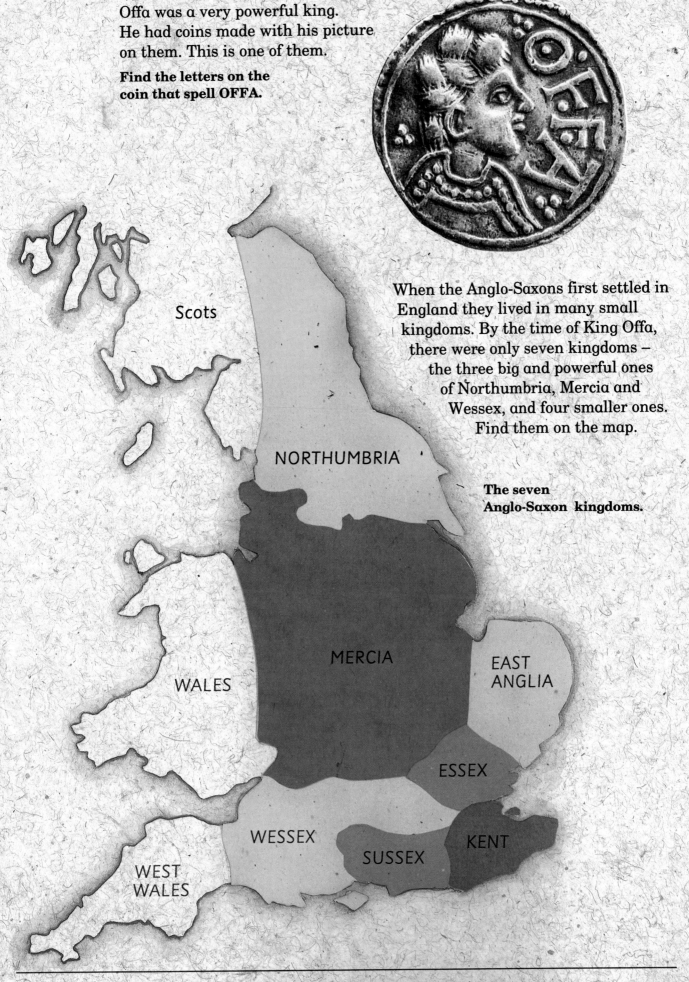

When the Anglo-Saxons first settled in England they lived in many small kingdoms. By the time of King Offa, there were only seven kingdoms – the three big and powerful ones of Northumbria, Mercia and Wessex, and four smaller ones. Find them on the map.

The seven Anglo-Saxon kingdoms.

Scots

NORTHUMBRIA

WALES

MERCIA

EAST ANGLIA

ESSEX

WESSEX

SUSSEX

KENT

WEST WALES

King Alfred and the Danes

This coin shows Alfred, King of Wessex. In Alfred's time news came that fierce **raiders** from the sea were attacking churches, villages and monasteries near the coast. They stole food, jewels, gold and silver.

Raiders
People who make a sudden attack on a place, stealing and causing damage.

Even their boats looked fierce. They had carved animals on them like this.

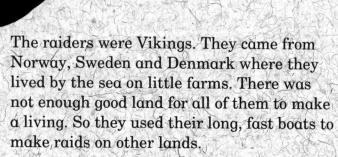

The raiders were Vikings. They came from Norway, Sweden and Denmark where they lived by the sea on little farms. There was not enough good land for all of them to make a living. So they used their long, fast boats to make raids on other lands.

They raided England for many years. Then some of them decided to settle. A large army of Vikings arrived from Denmark. The Anglo-Saxons called it the 'Great Army'. They called these Vikings 'Danes'.

The Great Army took over most of the Anglo-Saxon kingdoms. Then it marched into Wessex.

Alfred and his people fought nine battles against the Danes in one year. Then the Danish leader, Guthrum, agreed to go away and leave Wessex in peace.
Some of the Danes settled in Northumbria.

Five years later Guthrum attacked Wessex again. He took the Anglo-Saxons by surprise at Christmas when no-one expected fighting. Alfred had to hide in a secret **stronghold** in the middle of some marshes in Somerset.

Stronghold
A strongly defended place.

In the spring Alfred sent messages to his thanes telling them where to meet him with their men. Then they defeated the Danes in a fierce battle on Salisbury Plain.

Guthrum promised Alfred to take the Danes to live in East Anglia.
Look at the map and find where they settled.

All the Anglo-Saxons who lived outside the Danish settlements now thought of Alfred as their king.

The Rule of King Alfred

Alfred wanted to make Wessex stronger in case the Danes, or any other Vikings, attacked again. He ordered ships to be built.

They were even longer than Viking ships. He was the first English king to build a navy.

He also had twenty-nine royal towns built. They were called 'burhs'. Our word 'borough' come from 'burh'.

A burh had strong walls made of stone or earth. It was a fortress that the villagers living nearby could go to for safety if they were attacked.

Building a burh

It was also a safe place to hold the weekly market where people could come to buy and sell things.

You can still see the walls round some of Alfred's burhs. This is Wareham in Dorset.

Find the remains of the high earth walls. What else protects this town?

The Anglo-Saxons expected their kings to make **laws** and punish people who did wrong.

Here is a king judging cases with his chief thanes and **bishops**. The Anglo-Saxons called the people who helped the king the 'witan'.

| **Laws** |
| The laws of a country are the rules that everyone who lives there must obey. |

Bishop

A bishop is the priest in charge of all the priests and churches in a big area.
His own church is called a 'cathedral'.

Find:
- The king. The sword he is holding is called 'the sword of justice'. It shows that he makes laws and punishes people.

- The witan.

- The man being hanged for doing wrong.

Each Anglo-Saxon kingdom had slightly different laws. Alfred decided to make one set of laws for everyone. He had them written down so that everyone knew what they were.

Very few people could read and write in Alfred's time. Even he did not learn until he was grown up.

Alfred thought books and learning were important. He thought the thanes who helped him to rule should be able to read and write and know about the history of their people. So he set up a school in his palace for the sons of thanes.

Monks wrote in Latin. Alfred had some of their books turned into English so that more people could read them. One of these was Bede's *A History of the English Church and People*.

We use Bede's books today to find out about Anglo-Saxon times.

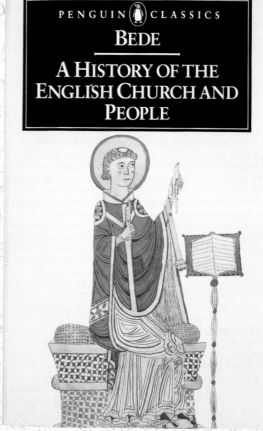

This gold jewel may have belonged to Alfred.
Find:

- The letters round the side. They say, 'Alfred had me made'.

- The animal head.

- The hole at the end. A long stick fitted in here to make a pointer for following the place in a book.

Queen Aethelflaed and King Edward

Alfred's eldest child was called Aethelflaed. She married the ruler of Mercia. When he died Aethelflaed became ruler. She was called 'First Lady of the Mercians'.

When Alfred died his son, Edward, became king of Wessex. Aethelflaed and Edward wanted to win back the Anglo-Saxon lands where the Danes were living.

They attacked the Danes together and won back nearly all the land. All the Anglo-Saxons and Danes in the south and middle of England obeyed Edward as their king.

King Athelstan and the Kingdom of England

Edward's son, Athelstan, finished off the job Aethelfaed and Edward had begun. He won back the last part of the Danish lands in the north of England.

So now there was only one Anglo-Saxon king, and he was ruler of all England.

King Athelstan holding a book

Art, Books and Buildings

You can still see many of the things the Anglo-Saxons made in museums today.

This helmet is in a museum in York. It is made of iron and brass. It must have belonged to an important Anglo-Saxon from a royal or noble family.

The person who made it was an artist as well as a metal-worker.

Find:
- **The flaps to protect the cheeks.**
- **The hinges for the flaps.**
- **The chain mail to protect the neck.**
- **The brass nose-piece.**
  Look at the patterns on it.

Two men found the helmet when they were working on a building site in York. Their mechanical digger hit something hard. They asked some archaeologists to come and look.

Here is the helmet just before the archaeologists took it away.

The archaeologists took five hours to clear away the earth around the helmet and to draw and photograph everything they found.

Then they took the helmet away. They cleaned it carefully and mended the broken bits.

Cleaning the helmet.

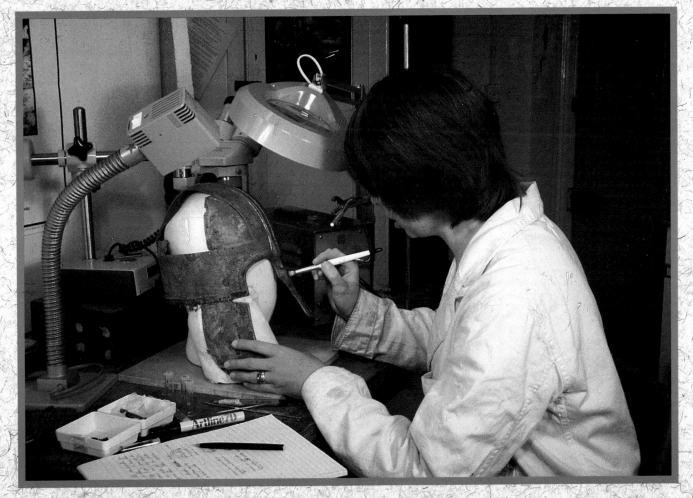

43

People still read the poems, stories and books which the Anglo-Saxons wrote.

This is a page from a book called the *Anglo-Saxon Chronicle* which you can see in the British Museum. A chronicle is a list of things that have happened.

King Alfred started the *Anglo-Saxon Chronicle*. He told monks to find out all they could about the history of the Anglo-Saxons in England and write it down. Then he told them to keep the chronicle up to date like a diary.

AN means year. Find the date beside it written in Roman figures.

Most Anglo-Saxon buildings fell down and rotted away long ago. But you can still see some of the churches they built out of stone.
Here is one.

Find out if there is a church near you with some Anglo-Saxon parts in it.

This is All Saints Church in Earls Barton in Northamptonshire. The Anglo-Saxons built the tower about a thousand years ago.

This is part of a piece of Anglo-Saxon embroidery. To see it, you have to go to a church in Bayeux in France.

It tells the story of how William, Duke of Normandy, invaded England in 1066 and defeated the Anglo-Saxon king, Harold, at the Battle of Hastings. William became the first Norman king of England.

William's brother Odo, who was Bishop of Bayeux, ordered English women to make this embroidery for him. It is called the Bayeux Tapestry. This scene show the Normans chasing the English after the Battle of Hastings.

Find:
- The Normans.
- The English.
- The dead bodies at the bottom.

Words, Names and Places

Many of the common words that we use in the
English language today come from Anglo-Saxon.

Here are some of them.

Our word	Anglo - Saxon word		
English	Englisc	lock	loc
England	Engle - land	red	read
king	cyning	out	ut
penny	penig	half	healf
high	heath	son	sunu
green	grene	dust	dust
hot	hat	hill	hill
cold	cald	kiss	cyssan

The Anglo-Saxons named some of the days of the week
after their gods and we still use those names:

Day of the week	Anglo - Saxon god
Tuesday	Tiw, god of war
Wednesday	Woden, chief god
Thursday	Thunor, god of sky and thunder
Friday	Frig, goddess of growing

Sunday and Monday
are named after the
sun and moon.
Saturday is named
after a Roman god
called Saturn.

We still use many of the names that the Anglo-Saxons
gave to places when they settled here.

You can find the names they used on page six.

Do any places near you have Anglo-Saxon names?

The Anglo-Saxon kings divided England up
into big areas called 'shires'.

This map shows the shires and tells you their names.

Many of our counties are the same as the shires.
Is your county an old Anglo-Saxon shire?

The Anglo - Saxon shires

—— The Anglo - Saxon shires

SCOTLAND

Northan Humbraland

Cumbraland

Dunholm

Westmoringaland

Eofordwic

ENGLAND

Luneceaster

Ceaster

Deoraby

Snottngham

Lincolne

Lygraceaster

Huntandune

Staefford

Northfolc

Scrob

Wigeraceaster

Northamtun

Grantan

Suthfolc

Waeringwic

WALES

Hereford

Gleavanceaster

Oxnaford

Bucchgaham

Heortford

Bedanford

Eastseaxe

Bearwuk

Middelseaxe

Wiltun

Sudridge

Cent

Sumursaetna

Hamtun

Suthseaxe

Defena

Dornsaetas

Cornwall

In the News

People are still finding things from Anglo-Saxon times.

This picture is from a newspaper telling how archaeologists found gold and silver jewellery in Anglo-Saxon graves in Norfolk.

Each new find gives us more clues about what the Anglo-Saxons were like and how they lived.

Some of the Anglo-Saxon gold and silver jewellery that has been unearthed from a seventh century graveyard in Norfolk
Photograph: Tony Hall

THE INDEPENDENT

Thursday 12 July 1990

Trevor Ashwin with a gold pendant found in one of the graves

Gold and silver legacy of Anglo-Saxon graveyard

By David Keys
Archaeology Correspondent

MAGNIFICENT gold and silver jewellery from the seventh century AD has been unearthed in Norfolk. Excavations next to the site of a Roman town outside Norwich yielded one of the finest collections of Anglo-Saxon gold and silver work found in Britain this century.

Thirty silver and gold jewellery items were discovered in a series of Anglo-Saxon graves 1,000 yards north-west of the site of Venta Icenorum, a Romano-British town which, after it had been deserted by the Romans, appears to have been used as a market place in the Dark Ages.

Forty graves were excavated, and a quarter yielded high qual-

ity jewellery. In one the corpse was wearing a gold pendant inlaid with garnets, and was buried with two silver coins and a little bronze sewing casket filled with pins and thread.

Another corpse had been interred wearing an oval Roman gemstone inscribed with the figure of a god set in a gold mount, while a third had a filigree gold pendant bearing a cross-shaped motif.

Silver items recovered range from finely-made pins and chains to a large brooch inlaid with gar-

nets. Many of those in the cemetery were interred with little leather and textile purses containing glass and faience beads, silver chains and iron keys.

Some material is so delicate that it has had to be removed still in its earth matrix for x-ray analysis at Norwich Castle Museum.

Several knives and buckles, and a short sword, have survived but all the bones have disintegrated because of the acid soils.

Most of those buried do not appear to have been warriors. They were almost certainly a mixed group of men, women and children.

Thirty-five of the 40 burials were in coffins and it appears

that all the deceased were interred wearing their best clothes and jewellery. All the graves were laid out in neat rows with the heads pointing due east.

The date of the cemetery, about AD 700, suggests that the graves belonged to Christians.

The excavation, which received £110,000 from English Heritage, is being directed by Trevor Ashwin of the local government-run Norfolk Archaeological Unit.

The discovery of the graves was unexpected and English Heritage's ancient monuments inspectorate rushed in extra financial assistance to enable proper excavations to take place.

The site — Bronze Age, Iron Age and Anglo-Saxon graves — is being excavated to rescue the archaeological evidence before the cemetery is destroyed in September by the construction of the Norwich southern bypass.